TITANIC
101

TITANIC 101

The Great Infographic History

Steve Hall

Infographics by Katie Beard

DOWNLOAD THE TITANIC APP

For the full *Titanic* experience visit The History Press website and follow the *Titanic* link www.thehistorypress.co.uk

For stories and articles about *Titanic*, join us on Facebook

First published 2013

The History Press
The Mill, Brimscombe Port
Stroud, Gloucestershire, GL5 2QG
www.thehistorypress.co.uk

British Library Cataloguing in Publication Data.
A catalogue record for this book is available from the British
Library.

ISBN 978 0 7524 9774 7

Typesetting and origination by The History Press
Printed in Great Britain

Contents

Acknowledgements

The author would like to acknowledge, with gratitude, the assistance of the following individuals:

Art Braunschweiger, George M. Behe, Bruce Beveridge, Mark Chirnside, Tad Fitch, Dave Gittins, Lester J. Mitcham, Captain Charles B. Weeks, Bill Wormstedt, Samuel Halpern, Cathy Akers-Jordan, Jonathan Smith, John White, Scott Andrews, Daniel Klistorner, The Titanic Historical Society, Ed and Karen Kamuda, Robert Hahn, Rene Bergeron, Stuart Kelly, Daniel Allen Butler and G. Michael Harris.

If we have unintentionally omitted credit to anyone for their contribution, we hope the omission will be forgiven. We will be glad to acknowledge anyone inadvertently left out in future reprintings where possible.

Introduction by Steve Hall

'*Titanic* is unsinkable.' This phrase strikes a chord in the mind of any *Titanic* enthusiast and is reiterated in nearly every *Titanic* story told. Yet no one from the shipyard that constructed the ship ever claimed the ship was 'unsinkable'. The period trade publication *The Shipbuilder* described *Titanic* and *Olympic* as '*practically* unsinkable'. Although it wasn't actually said in print, many people talked about the ship's unsinkability, including many employees both before the maiden voyage as well as on board.

From myth and fact to the mysteries of the ship's history, *Titanic*'s story has captured the world's attention for over a century. It is most often the odd or lesser known tidbits of information that people find the most fascinating. What was the weather like when *Titanic* departed Southampton on the start of her maiden voyage; how thick were the steel hull plates that formed the ship's skin; why did *Titanic* have four funnels when only three were required?

Until 1985, the wreck of *Titanic* was a much sought-after prize that many considered equal to the quest for the Holy Grail. With the discovery of the ship we now have confirmation that she did actually break apart. This fact opened further avenues of research into the events of that tragic night. Only in the last few decades, following the discovery of the wreck, have so many pieces of the puzzle started to fit together, giving us a fuller picture of the ship's 101-year history. Through diligent research, expeditions, documentaries and publications, the whole of the story has been revealed.

The ship itself was the latest in marine technology. Largest in the world, with opulent interiors, lavish appointments and facilities such as restaurants, a heated pool, gymnasium and Turkish baths, the latter being principally the domain of those travelling first class. This is not to say that second- or third-class (steerage) passengers' accommodation, dining rooms and public spaces were in any way lacking reasonable quality and comforts. A little-known fact is that many passengers who were rich enough to afford a White Star Line first-class ticket travelled second class by choice because it was less of a hassle. There was no need to change into full dress for supper, for instance!

All wasn't quite so rosy for third-class passengers on *Titanic*'s sister ship *Olympic* though. After breakfast, passengers were often encouraged to go topside or to one of the recreation rooms so that the stewards could clean their rooms. Sometimes this consisted of washing down the decks with a hose. With the fact that there were just two bathtubs for all of third class, this reminds us of how times have changed. But for most, their shared on-board accommodation was a step up from previous cottages and tenements they'd vacated.

But the story of this magnificent ship isn't just necessarily about how many rivets were used in the construction, nor how many propellers drove the ship across the Atlantic. It is about those who built the ship, the crew and passengers who sailed on her, and the rich tapestry of liner travel during the height of the Edwardian era.

Those on board were representative of the many different classes travelling beyond Queenstown to New York. For most travelling third class, their decision to emigrate was principally driven by the desire to obtain financial security, the abundant work opportunities available and, of course, the hopefulness of a better life.

Nearly everyone that boarded the ship shared a common sentiment; they did so with confidence and expectation of a safe voyage.

From lessons learnt following the disaster many new rules and regulations were introduced: ships at sea were to carry lifeboat provisions for all on board; the route from Queenstown to New York was moved further south to avoid icebergs and sea ice; and international sea patrols to monitor the sea lanes were introduced.

The ship today lies more than 12,000ft below the icy waters of the North Atlantic, nothing more than a crumpled and dismembered steel hulk. But the memory of the ship, her crew, passengers, shipyard and builders lives on. One hundred years from now her name and memory will still be remembered: forever linked with heroism, self-sacrifice and tragedy.

Steve Hall
NSW, Australia

STEVE HALL is an internationally renowned *Titanic* author. He has co-authored several landmark *Titanic* books which include *Titanic: The Ship Magnificent, Report into the Loss of the SS Titanic: A Centennial Reappraisal* and *Titanic in Photographs.*

Over the last decade his established expertise on the ship has seen him engaged as an advisor to auction houses, the media and museums around the world. Today he is one of the world's foremost authorities on *Titanic*'s design and general working arrangements, as well as a recognised authority on the technical aspects of the ship's construction.

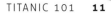

Design,
Construction
& Launch

It is generally believed that the concept for the *Olympic*-class liners was decided over dinner in Downshire House, the London residence of the then Harland and Wolff chairman Lord Pirrie, in the autumn of 1907. Present at the dinner was the White Star Line managing director J. Bruce Ismay.

The shipyard's chief draughtsman was Alexander Carlisle. It was to him, Roderick Chisholm and Thomas Andrews that Lord Pirrie appointed the task of designing the ships for construction. Carlisle would resign before completion of *Olympic*, and Chisholm and Andrews would both be lost in the sinking of *Titanic*.

Olympic and *Titanic* represented a 50 per cent increase in size over the Cunard vessels *Lusitania* and *Mauretania*, which were the largest and fastest liners in the world at that time.

The first to be built were *Olympic* and *Titanic*, side by side in 2 new slips, whereas the construction of the third sister, *Britannic*, did not begin until 3 years later.

The cost for the ships was £3 million for the pair. Harland and Wolff's arrangement with White Star Line for ship construction was by their usual terms, 'Cost plus 3 per cent'.

Titanic's keel was laid down on 31 March 1909. On the last day of May 1911, just after midday, the ship was launched. The outfitting of the great ship was complete by 31 March 1912.

After successfully completing her sea trials, *Titanic* departed Belfast for Southampton. She arrived late the following evening and docked alongside Berth 44 just after midnight.

001. Timeline: From Order to

30 APR **1907**	**31** MAR **1909**	**16** APR **1910**	**19** OCT **1910**	**31** MAY **1911**
★	★	★	★	★
★	★	★	★	★
★	★	★	★	★
★	★	★	★	★
★	★	★	★	★
★	★	★	★	★
★	★	★	★	★
★	★	★	★	★
★	★	★	★	★
★	★	★	★	★
★	★	★	★	★
★	★	★	★	★
★	★	★	★	
★	★	★	★	
★	★	★	★	
★	★	★	★	
★	★	★	★	

Order to proceed with construction was given

Construction was begun on Harland and Wolff's No. 3 slip

Frame completed

Plating completed

Titanic towered overhead in the gantry as more than 100,000 people turned out to see the spectacular event of her launch, which took place at 12.15 p.m. and lasted exactly 62 seconds*

*The same day *Titanic* was then moved to the Outfitting Wharf where the ship's heavy machinery such as her boilers and engines would be lowered into the hull

Trials

JAN **1912**	**3** FEB **1912**	**17** FEB **1912**	**1** APR **1912**	**2** APR **1912**

Lifeboats were fitted

The only know film of *Titanic* was captured on a short 1-minute newsreel, the day she entered the dry dock. This film is, to this day, the only known moving picture taken of the ship

Necessary work in dry dock was completed and she was removed and again shifted to the Outfitting Wharf

Planned sea trials were postponed due to the bitter weather turning the normally calm Victoria Channel rough and choppy

Returned to Belfast at 6.30 p.m. Board of Trade surveyor Francis Carruthers, being satisfied with the ship's performance throughout the trials, signed the certificate of sea-worthiness valid for 1 year

002. Build by Numbers

Titanic's hull number was 401: the official No. 131428.

003. Workforce

During the construction of *Titanic* and *Olympic*, the workforce at the shipyard had grown to well over 10,000. Approximately 6,000 men were directly involved with the building of the *Olympic*-class ships, about one-sixth of whom were on nightshift.

004. Paying the Men (but only just)

In 1911, skilled shipyard workers who built *Titanic* earned £2 per week. Unskilled workers earned £1 or less per week.

005. Mixed Designation

During construction *Titanic* was referred to as TSS: Triple Screw Ship. *Titanic* was later designated SS: Steam Ship. She was finally assigned the prefix RMS: Royal Mail Steamer.

006. Main Specifications

Length: 882ft 6in; breadth: 92ft 6in (max.); draft: 34ft 7in; displacement: 52,310; gross registered tonnage (GRT): 46,328.

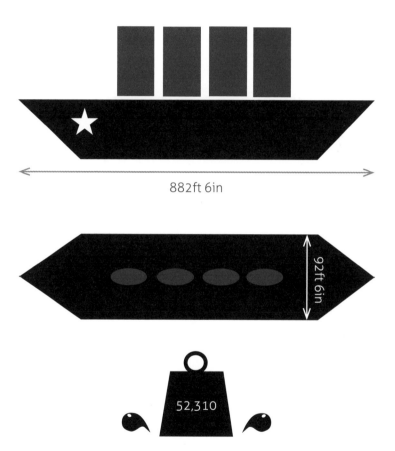

882ft 6in

92ft 6in

52,310

In looking at the weight of a ship, displacement is the amount of water dislocated. When the ship is loaded down to its approved draught (34ft 6in), then it will displace a calculated quantity of water.
GRT is a measure of enclosed space, not the weight of the ship.

The 31st of May 1911, will remain notable in the annals of shipbuilding and ship-owning as witnessing the launch of the Titanic and the departure from Belfast of the Olympic.

The Shipbuilder, 1911

The Titanic stood for the 'last word' in naval architecture. Not only did she carry to a far greater degree than any other ship the assurance of safety which we have come to associate with more size; not only did she embody every safeguard against accident known to the naval architect ... she was built at the foremost shipyard of Great Britain.

Scientific American, 27 April 1912

There was too much brag and not enough seaworthy construction.

Sir James Bisset

Workshop
007. Rivets

More than half a million rivets were used on *Titanic*'s double bottom, and the weight of these rivets alone was estimated to be 270 tons. When completed *Titanic* had about 3 million rivets with an estimated weight of over 1,200 tons.

1,200 tons

008. Rudder

Titanic was fitted with a cast-steel rudder, which weighed 101¼ tons, had an overall height of 78ft 8in and a width of 15ft 3in.

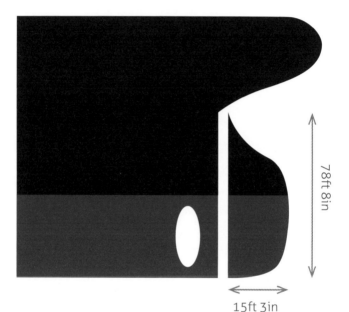

78ft 8in

15ft 3in

009. Horsepower

Titanic's impressive array of machinery was capable of generating up to 51,000hp combined.

010. Speed

Titanic's maximum speed was estimated to be 24 knots, with a cruising speed of 21 knots.

011. Boilers & Furnaces

Titanic had 29 huge boilers that comprised 159 furnaces. These furnaces had a heating surface of approximately 144,142 sq/ft. There were 24 double-ended boilers and 5 single-ended boilers.

012. Fossil Fuel

The ship's coal bunkers had a combined capacity of 6,611 tons and, operating at 21–22 knots, the ship could consume 620–640 tons of coal per day.

013. Let there be Light

There were literally hundreds of miles of electrical cable throughout this massive ship; the lighting alone was provided by approximately 10,000 incandescent lamps.

014. Anchors Away!

Titanic had 3 anchors with cast-steel heads. The starboard- and port-side anchors weighed 157cwt, 3qr, 8lb, or 7.89 long tons. The centre anchor was 316cwt or 15.80 long tons. At the time, *Titanic's* centre anchor – dimensions approx. 17ft long by 10ft 3in wide – was the largest in the world. The anchor cables, starboard and port were 3⅜in-diameter cable and 165 fathoms long, weighing 960cwt, 8lb.

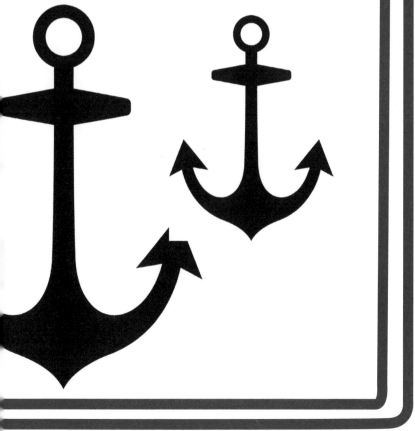

015. Propellers

The 2 outer propellers had a diameter of 23ft 6in. The centre propeller was 16ft 6in diameter.

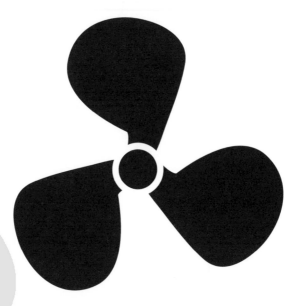

Infobit: Propellers

Titanic's wing propellers (port and starboard) were each 3-bladed, had a diameter of 23ft 6in and weighed a massive 38 tons. They were of 'built-up' construction, having manganese bronze blades bolted on to a cast-steel hub. The centre propeller had a diameter of 16ft 6in and weighed 22 tons. It had four blades and was cast as a single piece in manganese bronze. Because the turbine was not equipped to move in reverse, the centre propeller operated only in the 'ahead' direction.

016. Watertight

Titanic had 15 main watertight bulkheads, giving the ship 16 watertight compartments.

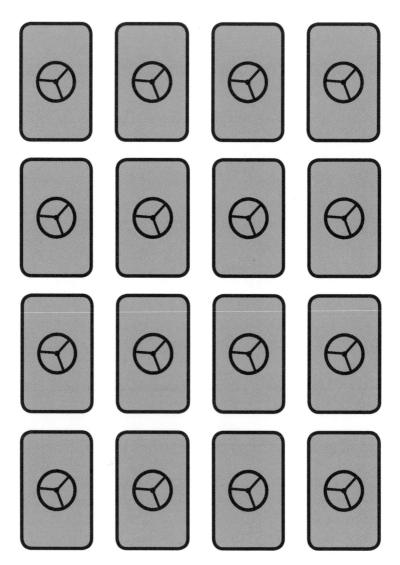

017. Lifeboat Complement

Titanic was fitted with 16 pairs of Welin davits, 8 on each side of the ship. Rigged under the davits were 16 wooden lifeboats: 14 30ft boats with a combined capacity of 910 persons (65 each), and 2 smaller emergency cutters (25ft 2in) with a combined capacity of 80 persons (40 each). The ship was also equipped with an additional 4 Engelhardt collapsible boats (27ft 5in long) with a combined capacity of 188 people (47 each).

018. Champagne Launch?

The ship was not christened with the breaking of a champagne bottle across the bow.

019. Portholes

Titanic had over 2,400 portholes.

020. Compasses

Titanic was equipped with 18 compasses.

021. All Mod Cons

Titanic had a Turkish bath, a gymnasium, a salt water swimming pool and a squash court. These were only available to first-class passengers.

022. Fine Dining

Titanic's culinary facilities were no less impressive. The first-class dining saloon could seat 554 passengers in one sitting, yet service did not suffer from such numbers: there was, on average, 1 steward for every 3 passengers. The galleys were immense and served everything from roast duckling to Waldorf pudding. Passengers ate off the finest Royal Crown Derby and Spode china and drank from Stuart crystal.

023. Sailing Palm Trees?

The Veranda Café had real palm trees.

024. Sheer Size

When completed, *Titanic* was the largest man-made moveable object in the world.

025. Expense

Olympic and *Titanic* cost £3 million for the pair.

026. Bells

The electric bell installation on *Titanic* comprised no less than 1,500 bell pushes throughout the ship.

027. Making a Call

The main telephone switchboard was located in a room just forward of the first-class elevators on C Deck, and was capable of handling 50 lines. These included the rooms of senior officers and various service rooms. A light activated on the switchboard when a call was incoming.

028. Passenger Elevators

Titanic's first- and second-class passengers were provided with lifts, or elevators. Second-class passengers had only 1 at their forward staircase, while first-class passengers had 3 located side by side immediately forward of the grand staircase.

029. Fire at Sea

There were 524 electric radiators provided throughout the ship and even an operational fireplace in the first-class smoke room. This fireplace was fuelled by coal and came equipped with all of the tools necessary for using it.

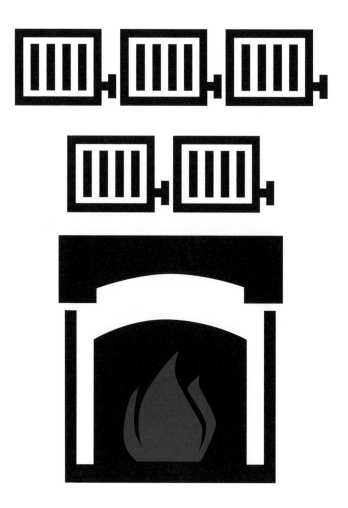

030. Tick Tock!

There were 48 clocks installed throughout the ship, which were slaved to a pair of master clocks secured within watertight cases in the chart room. The 2 master clocks worked in unison with each other, registering the exact same time.

031. Whistles & Funnels

Titanic was fitted with a set of steam whistles on each of the 4 funnels. Though all 4 sets appeared to be genuine, in fact only those mounted on the Nos 1 and 2 Funnels were operational; the ones mounted on the Nos 3 and 4 Funnels were dummies. The sound of *Titanic*'s whistles could be heard up to 8 miles away.

Infobit: **Funnels**

One of the most visible features of Titanic was her 4 massive funnels. The first 3 funnels vented combustion gases from the boilers, with the 4th being called a 'dummy', although it was actually designed to function as a ventilator. This dummy funnel was also intended to enhance and give balance to the profile of the ship; at the same time, it gave the impression of greater power and speed to those non-technical passengers who tended to judge and compare vessels by the number of funnels they carried. They were each 22ft wide and 62ft high.

The Voyage

On Wednesday 10 April, at 12.15 p.m., the mooring lines of *Titanic* were dropped and, with the assistance of 4 tugs, 2 positioned behind the ship's stern and 2 connected by hawsers on her starboard side, *Titanic* was slowly eased away from her berth at Southampton.

Titanic than steamed 77 nautical miles across the English Channel, arriving at the French port of Cherbourg that evening. After disembarking 24 passengers, a further 274 joined the ship. Just after 8 p.m. she departed for Queenstown (known today as Cobh) on the south coast of Ireland. *Titanic* anchored in Cobh harbour just before noon the following day, where a further 7 passengers disembarked and 113 joined the ship. It was just after 1.30 p.m. when *Titanic* weighed anchor for the last time and then steamed out into the Atlantic, tracking westward for New York. The maiden voyage had begun.

Throughout the crossing *Titanic* received numerous reports of ice drifting further south into the area of the Grand Banks. Although the ship was originally tracking along the correct course for that season of the year, Captain Smith decided during the crossing to take *Titanic* slightly further to the south to avoid this ice.

Over the following days, *Titanic* averaged 21 knots; the weather was relatively fine and the seas mostly moderate. By the evening of 14 April, the temperature had started to drop noticeably; the night sky was clear, the stars shone brightly and the sea was unusually calm.

032. Timeline: From Belfast on

2 APR 1912	4 APR 1912	10 APR 1912

8.00 p.m. Departed Belfast Lough. Briefly tracked eastward into the Irish Sea and made for Southampton. During the 570-nautical-mile trip (660 miles; 1,060km), the notable highlight was a short run at near maximum speed, reaching an impressive 23.5 knots

Just after midnight Secured alongside Berth 44 in Southampton

12 noon *Titanic* departs Southampton for Cherbourg

6.35 p.m. Arrives at the French port of Cherbourg after steaming 77 nautical miles (89 miles; 143km). In total, 24 passengers disembarked and 274 joined the ship

to the Atlantic

11
APR
1912

Just after 8 p.m.
Weighed anchor
and departed for
Queenstown, Ireland

11.30 a.m.
Arrived at
Queenstown (Cobh
harbour). In total,
7 passengers
disembarked and 113
joined the ship

1.30 p.m.
Weighed anchor
and departed on her
maiden crossing to
New York

033. Cost of Tickets, Southampton to New York

First class (parlour suite): as much as £870.
First class (berth): from £30 to £60 depending on which deck.
Second class: from £12 to £18 depending on cabin location.
Third class: from £3 to £8 depending on number of persons per cabin.

(Figures based on those for RMS Olympic)

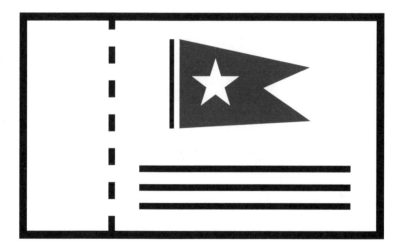

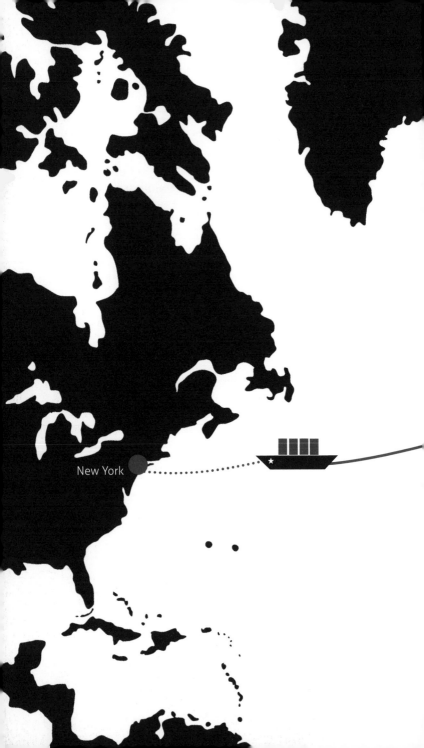

New York

034. The Voyage

Showing map from:
(1) Belfast to Southampton
(2) Southampton to Cherbourg
(3) Cherbourg to Queenstown (Cobh)
(4) From Queenstown heading westward to New York

Belfast

Queenstown

Southampton

Cherbourg

035. Passengers & Crew

When *Titanic* left Queenstown, there were: 1,317 passengers and 890 crew on board. Total: 2,207. Included in this number were: 9 members of the Guarantee Group from Harland and Wolff, 8 members of the ship's orchestra, 2 Marconi operators, 69 restaurant staff and 5 mail clerks.

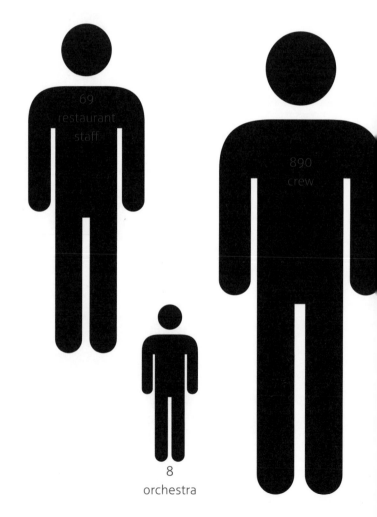

69 restaurant staff

8 orchestra

890 crew

9
Guarantee
Group

2
Marconi
operators

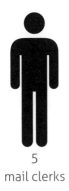

5
mail clerks

1,317
passengers

036. Radio Room

Cost to send a Marconi wireless telegram: 12 shillings and 6 pence for the first 10 words, and 9 pence per word thereafter. More than 250 passenger telegrams were sent and received during the voyage.

037. Distress Call

Titanic radio operators used both emergency call signs CQD (All Stations: Distress) and SOS (no literal 'translation').

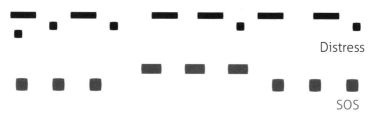

Distress

SOS

038. Money

There were 48 millionaires on board: the wealthiest passenger aboard was Lt Col John Jacob Astor IV, with a fortune estimated at about $100 million. He did not survive.

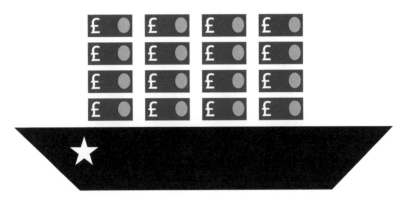

039. Capacity

Titanic had a passenger capacity of 3,547 fully loaded and had 1,317 passengers aboard on her maiden voyage.

040. Most Common Male Names

Robert

Edward

William

Thomas Ge

John

Joseph

Henry

Charles

orge

James

I never saw a wreck. I have never
been wrecked. I have never been in a
predicament that threatened to end
in disaster.

Captain Smith, *New York Times*, 1907

I have just been over the ship and seen all
the sitting- and saloon-rooms. It is all most
luxurious ... The decks are magnificent,
and the enclosed ones are fitted up more
like smoking-rooms. My cabin is not the
one shown ... on the Olympic plan ... It is,
however, more like a small bedroom than
a ship's cabin ... If only you could have got
safely to the ship, I know you would love to
have the voyage.

**Henry Forbes Junior,
first-class passenger, letter to his wife**

I herewith report this ship loaded and ready for sea. The engines and boilers are in good order for the voyage, and all charts and sailing directions up-to-date – Your obedient servant, Edward J. Smith.

Captain Smith,
Master's Report to Company

After dinner, we sat in the beautiful lounge listening to the White Star orchestra playing 'The Tales of Hoffman' and 'Cavalleria Rusticana' selections, and more than once we heard the remark 'You would never imagine you were on board a ship'.

Frank Browne, first-class passenger
(Ticket No. 84, £4)

041. Most Common Female Names

Helen

Erna

Margaret

Ma

Elizabe

Catherine

Ellen

nnie

ry

th

Alice

Marie

Maria

042. Most Common Surname

Fortune **Sage** Hart Ar

Smith

Thomas **Barker**

Davie

Evans **Phillips**

Goodwin Jones

Kelly Ward

Taylor

Johnson Carter

dersson Williams

Asplund Allen

Harris

Dean White

s Ford Rice

Brown

043. For The Dinner Plate

Fresh meat 75,000lb, fish 15,000lb, bacon and ham 7,500lb, poultry and game 25,000lb, fresh eggs 40,000, sausages 2,500lb, potatoes 40 tons, onions 3,500lb, tomatoes 3,500lb, fresh asparagus 800 bundles, fresh green peas 2,500lb, lettuce 7,000 heads, ice cream 1,750lb, coffee 2,200lb, tea 800lb, rice, dried beans etc. 10,000lb, sugar 10,000lb, flour 250 barrels, cereals 10,000lb, apples 36,000, oranges 36,000, lemons 16,000, grapes 1,000lb, grapefruit 13,000, jams and marmalade 1,120lb, fresh milk 1,500 gallons, fresh cream 1,200qts, condensed milk 600 gallons, fresh butter 6,000lb.

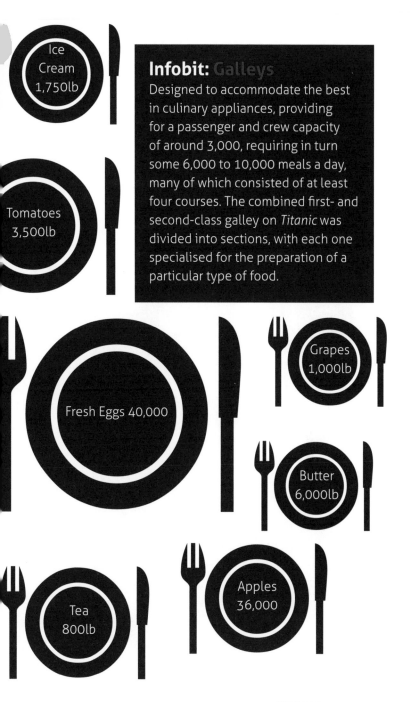

Ice Cream 1,750lb

Tomatoes 3,500lb

Infobit: Galleys

Designed to accommodate the best in culinary appliances, providing for a passenger and crew capacity of around 3,000, requiring in turn some 6,000 to 10,000 meals a day, many of which consisted of at least four courses. The combined first- and second-class galley on *Titanic* was divided into sections, with each one specialised for the preparation of a particular type of food.

Fresh Eggs 40,000

Grapes 1,000lb

Butter 6,000lb

Tea 800lb

Apples 36,000

044. Alcoholic Beverages

20,000 bottles of beer and stout, 1,500 bottles of wine, 8,000 cigars taken on board as stores. First-class passengers only!

045. Water

14,000 gallons of pure drinking water were used every 24 hours.

046. For Comfort

Blankets: 7,500, bed covers: 3,600, eiderdown quilts: 800,
single sheets: 15,000, bath towels: 7,500, fine towels: 25,000,
roller towels: 3,500, double sheets: 3,000, pillow-slips: 15,000.

Eiderdown Quilts

Double Sheets

Roller Towels

Bed Covers

Bath Towels

Blankets

Pillow-slips

Single Sheets

Fine Towels

047. For the Table

57,600 items of crockery, 29,000 pieces of glassware, including tea cups (3,000); plates (18,700), wine glasses (2,000), salt shakers (2,000), oyster forks (1,000), nut crackers (300), grape scissors (1,500), asparagus tongs (400), table cloths: 6,000, table napkins: 45,000, pieces of cutlery: 44,000.

57,600 items of crockery

29,000 pieces of glassware

44,000 pieces of cutlery

048. Accommodation

Staterooms: 840
First Class: 416
Second Class: 162
Third Class: 262 plus 40 open berthing areas

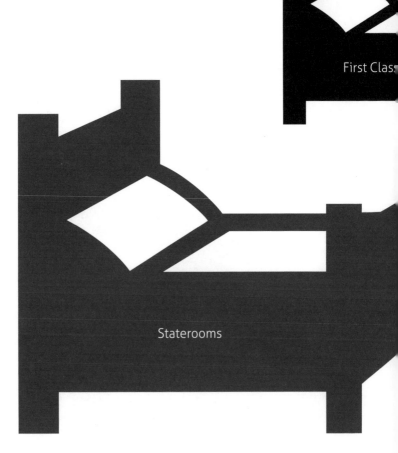

First Class

Staterooms

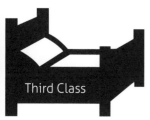
Third Class

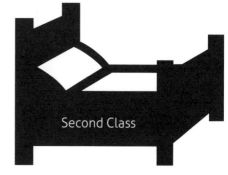
Second Class

Infobit: Special Staterooms

On B and C Decks were the 'special staterooms' of unparalleled luxury that *Olympic* and *Titanic* were so famous for. Brochures, magazines and newspapers all boasted of the 11 luxurious styles in which the various bedrooms and sitting rooms were decorated. These were: the Adam style; Italian Renaissance; Georgian; Regency; Empire; Louis Quatorze (Louis XIV); Louis Quinze (Louis XV); Louis Seize (Louis XVI); Queen Anne; Modern Dutch; and Old Dutch. While this is an impressive array of popular styles from centuries past, the number is made even more impressive by designs created by variations of many of these styles.

049. Lifebelts and Buoys

Titanic carried 3,560 lifebelts of the latest improved overhead pattern. They were distributed throughout the sleeping accommodations, or in metal lockers located in the alleyways. She also carried 49 life buoys.

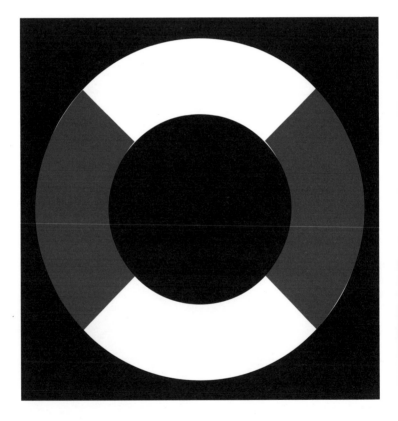

050. Love On Board

There were 13 honeymooning couples on board.

051. Seasickness

There were 2 seasickness cures available for ailing guests: beef tea or smelling salts.

052. Captain's Table

There was room for 6 esteemed guests at the captain's table.

Infobit:
First-class Dining

Titanic's first-class dining saloon on D Deck could seat 554 persons at one time, with one server usually assigned to every three persons. Between the main dining saloon and the à la carte restaurant, all first-class passengers could normally be accommodated in one sitting. The doors opened at 8 a.m. for breakfast on the westbound voyage and 8:30 a.m. on the eastbound voyage, and continued through until 10 a.m. Luncheon began at 1 p.m. westbound and at 1.15 p.m. eastbound, lasting through the afternoon. Tea was at 4 p.m. and dinner at 7 p.m. in either direction.

053. Key Players

The captain of *Titanic* was Edward J. Smith. He went down with the ship.

Thomas Andrews was managing director of Harland and Wolff. He went down with the ship.

J. Bruce Ismay was managing director of White Star Line. He managed to get a place aboard a lifeboat and survived to the age of 74, dying of a stroke in 1937.

054. Crew Salaries per month

Captain E.J. Smith, *Titanic*: £105
Captain Rostron, *Carpathia*: £53
Seaman Edward Buley: £5
Lookout G.A. Hogg: £5 and 5 shillings
Radio Operator Harold Bride: £48
Steward Sidney Daniels: £3 and 15 shillings
Stewardess Annie Robinson: £3 and 10 shillings

Steward
Sidney Daniels

Stewardess
Annie Robinson

Radio
Operator
Harold
Bride

Lookout
G.A. Hogg

Seaman
Edward Buley

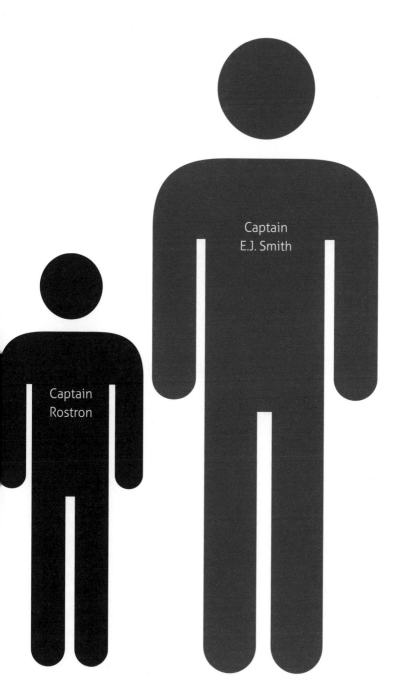

Captain
E.J. Smith

Captain
Rostron

055. Bathtubs

Only 2 promenade suites in first class had private bathrooms; third class had only 2 bathtubs for more than 709 passengers.

Infobit: Promenading

Promenading was as much a social activity as for exercise and fresh air. It was de rigueur for first-class passengers, and was as much about being seen as it was to see other people. The Promenade Deck, being sheltered and entirely reserved for first class, was the most popular for promenading and enjoying the outdoor air in deckchairs. Overhead battens were fitted at the deck head, on which were marked numbers corresponding to brass plates fastened to the chairs themselves. These numbers indicated the location of each individual chair, and saved the passengers the trouble of finding their chairs when they were covered with blankets or steamer rugs. The teak deckchairs, or steamer chairs, were hired at a cost of $1 or 4 shillings each.

056. Mail

Titanic had on board 3,500 sacks of mail. As the standard ocean mail bag held approximately 2,000 letters, it is estimated that in all there were about 7 million pieces of mail. The post office was on G Deck and manned by five postal clerks; two British and three American. At capacity, upwards of 60,000 items were sorted daily.

057. Cargo

Titanic was primarily a passenger liner, but carried specific amounts of cargo and goods.

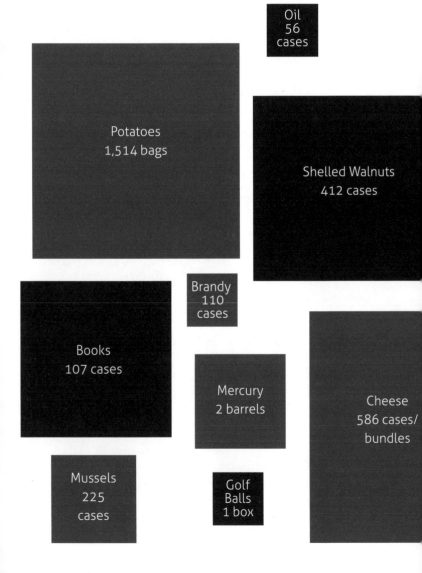

Oil
56
cases

Potatoes
1,514 bags

Shelled Walnuts
412 cases

Brandy
110
cases

Books
107 cases

Mercury
2 barrels

Cheese
586 cases/
bundles

Mussels
225
cases

Golf
Balls
1 box

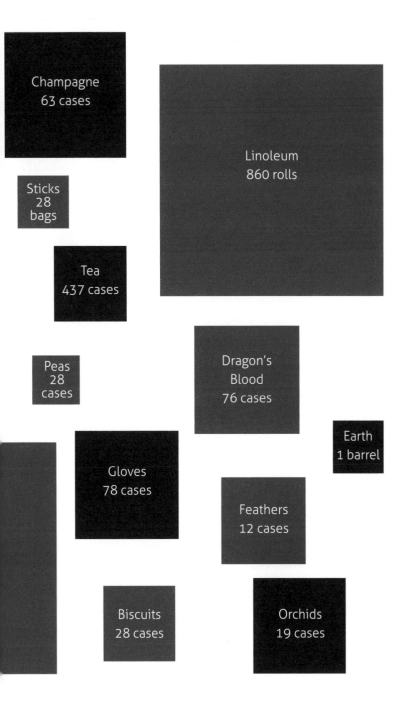

Champagne
63 cases

Linoleum
860 rolls

Sticks
28
bags

Tea
437 cases

Peas
28
cases

Dragon's
Blood
76 cases

Earth
1 barrel

Gloves
78 cases

Feathers
12 cases

Biscuits
28 cases

Orchids
19 cases

Cargo Capacities by Hatch and Type

HATCH NUMBER	TYPE
Fore:	
1	General cargo
2	General cargo and motorcars
3	First- and second-class baggage
3	Mail, parcels and specie
Aft:	
4	Uninsulated stores
4	Insulated (refrigerated) stores
5	Insulated (refrigerated) cargo
6	General cargo and third-class baggage
6	Potato stores (insulated)

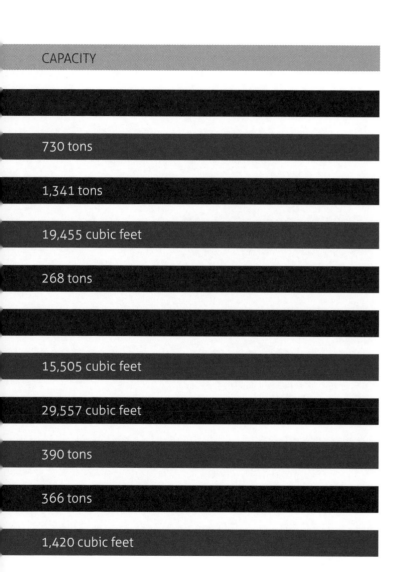

CAPACITY

730 tons

1,341 tons

19,455 cubic feet

268 tons

15,505 cubic feet

29,557 cubic feet

390 tons

366 tons

1,420 cubic feet

Impact & Sinking

At around 11.36 p.m. on 14 April 1912 lookout Fredrick Fleet spotted something directly ahead. Moments later he recognised it as an iceberg! He hailed the bridge: 'Iceberg directly ahead,' he called down the phone. First Officer Murdoch ordered the helm 'Hard a starboard'. The ship didn't have enough time to manoeuvre around the iceberg, however, and the ship struck along her starboard side. The collision damaged the hull below the waterline through 6 watertight compartments. *Titanic* was designed to remain afloat with 4 breached compartments, but not 6. On inspection, Thomas Andrews, the ship's chief designer, calculated the flooding rates and advised Captain Smith that the ship was doomed and would certainly sink.

At 12.27 a.m. the captain instructed Radio Operator Jack Phillips to start sending out a distress call, a CQD. The eastbound steamer *Carpathia* heard CQD at 12.37 a.m. and Captain R. Rostron turned his ship for *Titanic*'s position.

Lifeboat No. 7 was the first away at 12.40 a.m. and several minutes later *Titanic*'s fourth officer, Boxhall, fired off the first distress rocket.

By 2.17 a.m. the ship's stern was well clear of the water. The ship's lights that had remained on throughout suddenly went out, flashed back on momentarily, then off again. It is at this time *Titanic* broke in two. The stern section remained afloat for a further 3 minutes, then went under.

The first lifeboat came alongside *Carpathia* at 4.10 a.m. and the last at 8.15 a.m. With all 712 survivors on board (1,496 missing), *Carpathia* swept the area for any other survivors. With none found, she then steamed to New York, arriving on the evening of 18 April.

058. Timeline: Lead Up to the

14
APR
1912

9 a.m.
Reports of ice by
eastbound liner
Caronia

11.40 a.m.
Further reports of ice
by *Noordam*

1.42 p.m.
Further reports of ice
250 miles ahead of
Titanic by *Baltic*

1.45 p.m.
Further reports
of ice by *Baltic*

7.30 p.m.
Californian's
report of ice
is not passed
on to Captain
Smith

9.30 p.m.
Mesaba warns
of heavy
packice

11.36 p.m.
Titanic lookout
sees iceberg
and rings
warning bell;
evasive action
is taken

059. Watertight Doors

Titanic had 12 watertight doors. The time required to fully close the doors was between 25 and 30 seconds, and they would close automatically if water reached them.

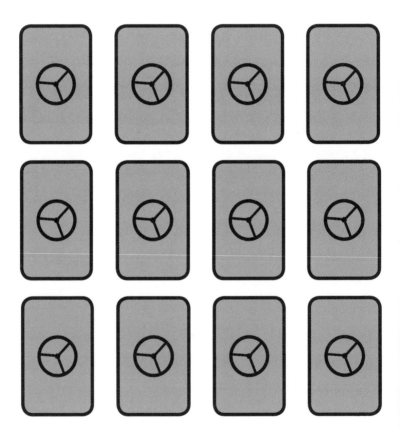

060. Flooded

The ship could have stayed afloat had only 4 compartments flooded. 6 became flooded.

061. Speed at Impact

22.5 knots.

062. Look Out!

It took *Titanic* 37 seconds to turn the vital 2 points to port, meaning split-second thinking was required by officers once the lookout had called out the alert.

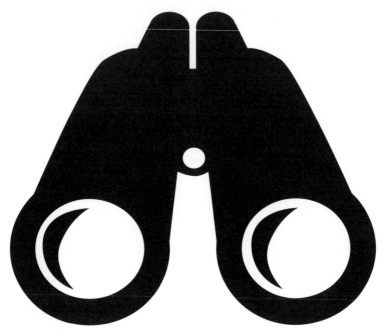

063. Land ahoy?

The ship was 400 miles (640km) from land when the iceberg was struck.

064. Iceberg

The iceberg was about 100ft tall. At 32°F, the iceberg was warmer than the water *Titanic* passengers fell into that night. The ocean waters were 28°F below freezing point but not frozen because of the water's salt content.

Myth Busting

065. Hull Wounds

There is not a huge gash in the hull.

066. Last Music

The last song the musicians played was likely to have been *Songe d'Automne*, not *Nearer My God to Thee*, though evidence suggests that both songs were played.

067. Pet Pigs

It was thought that Edith Russell had a pet pig on board *Titanic*. The pig, her lucky mascot, was in fact a toy, not a real animal.

068. Unsinkable?

No one ever stated in print that the ship was 'unsinkable'. The only written quotation along these lines was, 'She is practically unsinkable'.

069. Competition

Titanic's rivals, *Lusitania* and *Mauretania*, typically covered the same distance as *Titanic* in 116 hours. The idea that *Titanic*'s captain ignored the iceberg warnings because he was trying to set a new time record is one of many myths that endure.

070. *Titanic* Didn't Sink!

One theory suggests that *Titanic* was switched with her sister ship *Olympic* and deliberately sunk. This has been disproved by items recovered from the wreck.

071. Act of Sinking

As the ship was sinking, the stern rose out of the water and broke into 2 pieces between the 3rd and 4th funnels.

April 14: Sunday today it is raining and everybody must stay inside. There are all kinds of nationalities here among others Turks and Japanese.

Jakob Johansson, third-class passenger

COLLISION WITH ICEBERG – Apr 14 – Lat 41 degrees 46', lon 50 degrees 14', the British steamer TITANIC collided with an iceberg seriously damaging her bow; extent not definitely known.

J.J. Knapp, US Navy hydrographer

We were hit by an iceberg. We were in the midst of a field of ice, towers of ice: fantastic shapes of ice.

Alice Leader, first-class passenger

Imagine that on Sunday night we woke up to a dangerous noise, the ship hit an iceberg. We all got up, imagine the panic, but still we didn't think that she would go down. She was the biggest steamship in the world.

Olga Lundin, second-class passenger

072. Third-Class Prison

Third-class passengers were not locked in their accommodation during the sinking.

Infobit: All About Class

One myth that persists to this day is that of locked gates extending from floor to ceiling between the third-class areas and the rest of the ship. It must be noted that there is no evidence, either documented or from the wreck, other than survivor anecdotes that any such barriers existed. Although segregation of emigrants was required by United States immigration laws in order to prevent the spread of infectious diseases, this was accomplished far more by existing social barriers than any other means. Bostwick gates and other physical forms of separation were in place at various locations throughout the vessel, but their primary purpose was to clearly mark points through which third-class passengers could not pass, as many could not read. Gates were not intended, nor were they constructed, as a means of forcible confinement or physical restriction.

073. Timeline: The Sinking

14 APR **1912**

15 APR **1912**

11.40 p.m.
Moment of
impact

12.10 a.m.
First distress
calls sent
'CQD, MGY,
SOS'

12.25 a.m.
Order to put
women and
children into
lifeboats

12.40 a.m.
First lifeboat
(No. 7) lowered
with only 28 of
65 aboard

★
★
★
★
★
★
★
★
★
★
★
★
★
★
★
★
★
★
★
★
★
★
★

1.45 a.m.
Last message
to *Carpathia*:
'Engine room full
up to boilers'

★
★
★
★
★
★
★
★
★
★
★
★
★

2.20 a.m.
Titanic
disappears
beneath the
sea

★
★
★
★
★
★
★
★
★
★
★
★
★
★
★
★
★
★
★
★
★

4.10 a.m.
First lifeboat is
picked up
(No. 2)

★
★
★
★
★
★
★
★
★
★
★
★

8.15 a.m.
Last lifeboat is
picked up
(No. 12)

074. First Lifeboat Launch

Lifeboat No.7 was the first to be launched at 12.40 a.m. (65 minutes after hitting the iceberg). It carried 28 people yet was rated to hold 65.

075. Previously

During the 10 years previous to *Titanic*'s sinking, 2,179,594 passengers had been carried by the White Star Line. 2 of these had been killed during that period.

076. Going Down

Titanic dropped more than 2.5 miles to the ocean floor and took 5–7 minutes after it had submerged to do so.

077. Life Expectancy

The average life expectancy for *Titanic* victims in the water was 15–45 minutes.

078. SS *Carpathia*

Carpathia rescued 712 persons (call sign: MPA).

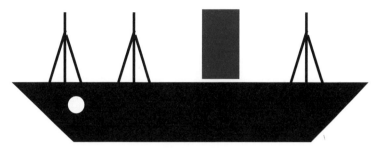

079. Engineering Staff

All engineering staff of both White Star and Harland and Wolff were lost in the disaster.

080. Lifeboat Launch & Arrival

Boat No. 1	Launched: 1.05 a.m.
Boat No. 2	Launched: 1.45 a.m.
Boat No. 3	Launched: 12.55 a.m.
Boat No. 4	Launched: 1.50 a.m.
Boat No. 5	Launched: 12.43 a.m.
Boat No. 6	Launched: 1.10 a.m.
Boat No. 7	Launched: 12.40 a.m.
Boat No. 8	Launched: 1.00 a.m.
Boat No. 9	Launched: 1.30 a.m.
Boat No. 10	Launched: 1.50 a.m.
Boat No. 11	Launched: 1.35 a.m.
Boat No. 12	Launched: 1.30 a.m.
Boat No. 13	Launched: 1.40 a.m.
Boat No. 14	Launched: 1.25 a.m.
Boat No. 15	Launched: 1.41 a.m.
Boat No. 16	Launched: 1.20 a.m.
Collapsible A	Floated Off: 2.15 a.m.
Collapsible B	Floated Off: 2.15 a.m.
Collapsible C	Launched: 2.00 a.m.
Collapsible D	Launched: 2.05 a.m.

*Of the 18 lifeboats that arrived at *Carpathia*, only 13 of them were taken back to New York. They were stored at White Star Line's Pier 59 and their contents inventoried in a 4-page report by C.M. Lane Lifeboat Co. of Brooklyn, NY. The recovered

Arrived (approx.): 4.45 a.m.

Arrived (approx.): 4.10 a.m.

Arrived (approx.): 7.30 a.m.

Arrived (approx.): 8.00 a.m.

Arrived (approx.): 6.00 a.m.

Arrived (approx.): 8.00 a.m.

Arrived (approx.): 6.15 a.m.

Arrived (approx.): 7.30 a.m.

Arrived (approx.): 6.15 a.m.

Arrived (approx.): 8.00 a m.

Arrived (approx.): 7.00 a.m.

Arrived (approx.): 8.15 a.m.

Arrived (approx.): 6.30 a.m.

Arrived (approx.): 7.15 a.m.

Arrived (approx.): 7.30 a.m.

Arrived (approx.): 6.45 a.m.

Later Abandoned

Later Abandoned

Arrived (approx.): 5.45 a.m.

Arrived (approx.): 7.15 a.m.

lifeboats brought back by *Carpathia* were Nos 1, 2, 3, 5, 6, 7, 8, 9, 10, 11, 12, 13 and 16.

(Halpern, Sam et al., Loss of the SS Titanic: A Centennial Reappraisal*)*

Loss of Life

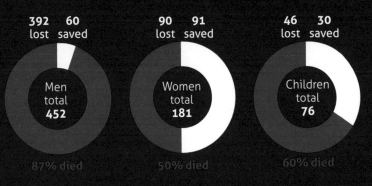

First Class

118 **58**
lost saved

4 **139**
lost saved

1 **4**
lost saved

Men
total
176

Women
total
143

Children
total
5

67% died

3% died

20% died

Second Class

154 **13**
lost saved

12 **83**
lost saved

0 **22**
lost saved

Men
total
167

Women
total
95

Children
total
22

92% died

13% died

0% died

Third Class

392 **60**
lost saved

90 **91**
lost saved

46 **30**
lost saved

Men
total
452

Women
total
181

Children
total
76

87% died

50% died

60% died

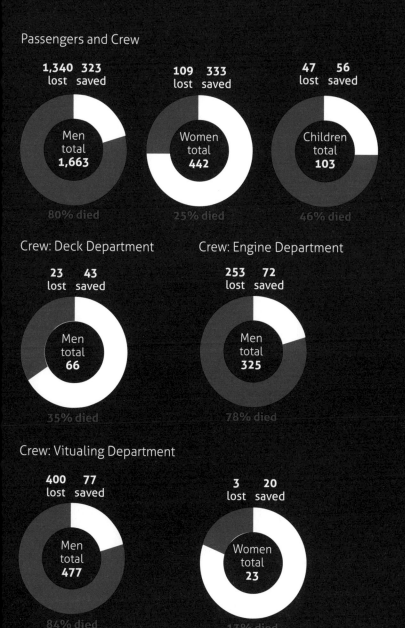

Passengers and Crew

1,340 **323**
lost saved

Men
total
1,663

80% died

109 **333**
lost saved

Women
total
442

25% died

47 **56**
lost saved

Children
total
103

46% died

Crew: Deck Department

23 **43**
lost saved

Men
total
66

35% died

Crew: Engine Department

253 **72**
lost saved

Men
total
325

78% died

Crew: Vitualing Department

400 **77**
lost saved

Men
total
477

84% died

3 **20**
lost saved

Women
total
23

13% died

Mr. Andrews met his fate like a true hero, realising the great danger, and gave up his life to save the women and children of the Titanic. They will find it hard to replace him, and I am terribly cut up about him.

Mary Sloan, stewardess

I jumped out, feet first, went down, and as I came up I was pushed away from the ship by some force. I was sucked down again, and as I came up I was pushed out again and twisted around by a large wave.

17-year-old Jack Thayer

I had no difficulty in filling the boat. The people were perfectly ready and quiet. There was no jostling or pushing or crowding whatever ... They could not have stood quieter if they had been in church.

2nd Officer Charles Lightoller, in charge of loading port-side lifeboats

No more could be seen of that grand ship; all was silent for a moment and then the cries of 1600 men. All were crying for help; it was terrible.

Robertha Watt, second-class passenger

082. Saviours

Only 2 lifeboats saved people from the water after being launched and 9 people were rescued from the water (3 of whom died shortly afterwards).

083. Pet Rescue

3 of 10 dogs were saved from *Titanic*, thought to be
2 Pomeranians and a Pekinese. There had been no lucky
cats on board.

084. Mystery Ship

A nearby vessel could be seen off the port side of *Titanic* at around 12.27 a.m., but the ship's identity remains a mystery. The ship probably was *Californian*. Had it responded, the ship would likely have arrived in time to save many *Titanic* passengers.

085. Bodies

Only 306 bodies of lost *Titanic* passengers were recovered, including 3 in a lifeboat found drifting almost a month after the disaster.

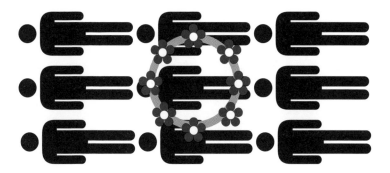

086. Musicians

The musicians played for 2 hours and 5 minutes from 12.20 a.m, and all went down with the ship.

087. Claimed Lost

1 Renault 35hp automobile owned by passenger William Carter.

1 Marmalade Machine owned by passenger Edwina Trout.

50 cases of toothpaste for Park & Tilford.

96 tennis balls which were to go to R.F. Downey & Co.

5 grand pianos.

1 jewelled copy of *The Rubáiyát* by Omar Khayyám, with illustrations by Eliku Vedder, sold for £405 at auction in March 1912 to an American bidder. The binding took 2 years to execute, and the decoration comprised 1,500 precious stones, each separately set in gold.

4 cases of opium.

I went on deck and met a sailor who asked me to help him lower the boats. The sailor said, 'Take a chance yourself.' I did, as did my friend, but the officers came along and ordered us off the boat. A woman said, 'Lay down, lad, you are somebody's child.' She put a rug over me and the boat went out, so I was saved.

Daniel Buckley, third-class passenger

Experience is great – I am fine and dandy – never better. What time did you hear of the disaster? I AM SO GLAD I WAS IN IT. I shall never forget it. We are just in New York. Having a jolly time. Don't worry.

Bertha Mulvihill, third-class passenger

We rowed off a ways and in less than an hour there was a mighty explosion. The boilers had exploded and the ship was broken right in two, and then, my dear, the screams and the shrieks as 1000 of the steerage went down, and I suppose, the crew and the officers and all the Americans. All my life I will hear those shrieks.

Kornelia Andrews, first-class passenger

Never had a morning appeared to me to be more beautiful than that of April 15th, and all the sadness of the last few hours was forgotten as we rowed towards the steamer in the icy morning wind ... Within a quarter of an hour Mr Simonius and his friend also arrived, and we were greatly relieved.

Hedwig Frolicher, first-class passenger

088. Other Passenger Ship Losses

4,341 – *Doña Paz* (1987)
1,800 – *Le Joola* (2002)
1,800 – *Sultana* (1865)
1,523 – *Titanic* (1912)
1,153 – *Toya Maru* (1954)
1,012 – *Empress of Ireland* (1914)
1,000 – *Al Salam Boccaccio 98* (2006)

089. Final Resting Place

The wreck is sited 1,000 miles due east of Boston, Massachusetts, and 375 miles south south-east off St John's, Newfoundland.

Location of bow section: 49° 56' 49" W, 41° 43' 57" N
Location of stern section: 49° 56' 54" W, 41° 43' 35" N
Approx. surface location where *Titanic* sank:
49° 56' 49" W, 41° 43' 32" N

090. Wreckage

Titanic lies approx. 12,460ft (2.5 miles) down, at the bottom of the Atlantic Ocean. She is resting in 2 main sections approx. 1 mile apart.

Post-Wreck

Following the loss of *Titanic* 2 inquiries were held: the US Senate Inquiry held between 19 April and 25 May 1912 and the British Inquiry between 2 May and 3 July the same year.

As a consequence of these inquiries there were several recommendations made: that wireless equipment on all passenger ships be manned around the clock; that sufficient lifeboats be provided for all on board; and that the requirement of scheduled lifeboat drills be strictly adhered to. It also saw the introduction of (an international) ice patrol to monitor the presence of icebergs in the North Atlantic, as well as the updating of maritime safety regulations.

The wreck of *Titanic* was finally discovered on 1 September 1985 by a joint French-American expedition led by Jean-Louis Michel of IFREMER and Robert Ballard of the Woods Hole Oceanographic Institution. It is located approximately 370 miles (595km) south-south-east off the coast of Newfoundland, lying on a gently sloping plain at a depth of about 12,460ft (3,797m). The ship lies in 2 main sections: the 450ft (136.16m) bow section, separated by 1,700ft (518m) from that of the 350ft (106m) stern section.

The discovery of the wreck in 2 sections appears to confirm witness statements that the ship seemed to break apart prior to sinking.

It is estimated that it took each separated section of the hull 5–6 minutes to reach the ocean floor.

091. Timeline: The Legacy

18 APR **1912**	**19** APR **1912**	**25** MAY **1912**	**2** MAY **1912**	**3** JUL **1912**

Carpathia arrives in New York with survivors

The American Inquiry, led by Sen. William Alden Smith

The British Inquiry, overseen by High Court Judge Lord Mersey mainly at the Royal Scottish Drill Hall, on Buckingham Gate, London

| 1959 | 1 SEP 1985 | 31 MAR 2012 | 12 APR 2012 |

★
★
★
★
★
★
★
★
★
★
★
★
★
★
★
★
★
★
★
★
★

Titanic Relief
Fund is wound
up

Wreck is
discovered

Titanic Belfast
opens

Centenary
celebrations
worldwide
including
Titanic
memorial
cruise to her
wreck site

092. Rescuers

Carpathia

Line:	Cunard
Captain:	Capt. Arthur Rostron
Recovery of 18 lifeboats:	No. 2 (first) at 4.10 a.m. and No. 12 (last) at 8.15 a.m.
Arrival at New York:	18 April, Pier 54
Fate:	Sunk by German U-boat *U-55*, 17 July 1918

Californian

Line:	Leyland Line
Captain:	Capt. Stanley Lord
Fate:	Sunk by German U-boat *U-35*, November 1915

093. Ownership of the Wreck

After a series of court battles, an American company, RMS Titanic Inc. (RMST), emerged as the owner of the salvage rights, allowing it to keep possession and put on touring display the 5,900 artefacts it has since lifted from the ship during 6 dives, but the company does not own the ship.

094. Cost Today

The estimated cost to rebuild the ship new today would be between £400 million and £600 million.

095. In the Press

The British newspaper, the *London Daily Mail*, reported 'Titanic Sunk, No Lives Lost', in its initial 16 April 1912 story. The *New York Times* devoted 75 pages to coverage of *Titanic* in the first week after the sinking.

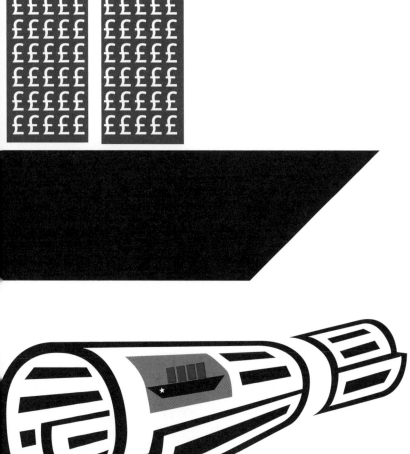

096. Inquiry

Titanic was carrying 20 lifeboats (enough for 1,178 people); she was required by law at the time to carry 16 lifeboats (enough for *c.* 1,040 people); the inquiry would change the requirement to carry enough for a ship's full capacity of passengers (enough for 3,547 peple or about 60 lifeboats for *Titanic*) (*Titanic*'s sister RMS *Olympic*'s lifeboat quota went up from 20 to 64 lifeboats).

No lifeboat drills were carried out on *Titanic*'s voyage, which would be required in future.

All rockets fired were now to be interpreted as a sign of distress.

The inquiry also led to the establishment of the International Ice Patrol.

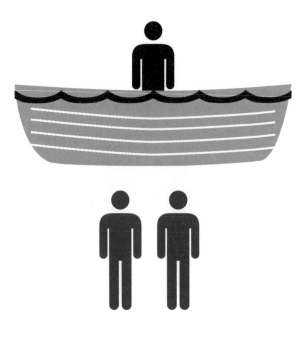

097. Relief

The official *Titanic* Relief Fund raised approximately £413,000 for the survivors of the disaster.

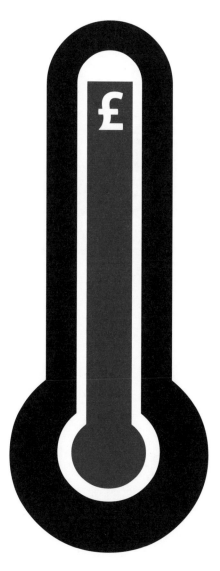

098. Rediscovery

Dr Robert Ballard of Woods Hole Oceanographic Institute, in a mission jointly led by Ballard and Jean-Louis Michel of IFREMER, found the wreck in September 1985, almost 74 years after *Titanic* sank.

099. Last Survivor

Since the death of Millvina Dean on 31 May 2009, there are no longer any living survivors of the *Titanic* tragedy. Millvina Dean was just 9 weeks old at the time of *Titanic*'s sinking.

Titanic, name and thing, will stand as a monument and warning to human presumption.

Bishop of Winchester, 1912

We've booked this once in a lifetime event as we wish to commemorate our relative, Mr Thomas Pears, who died on the *Titanic* and his story has been a big part of our lives.

Jane Allen, Devon, on the Titanic memorial cruise, 2012

My grandfather worked at Harland & Wolff so he helped to build the *Titanic*, but it wasn't ever spoken about much when I was growing up. Those who worked on building the ship took the disaster very personally and it was like a death in the family. He didn't want to talk about it.

Dennis Nightingale, Co. Antrim, 2012

We remember all those who perished ... – men, women and children – who loved and were loved, their loss still poignantly felt by their descendants.

Rev. Ian Gilpin, 2012

100. In Pop Culture

The film *Saved from the Titanic* was released only 29 days after the disaster in 1912.

Thomas Hardy composed 'The Convergence of the Twain (Lines on the loss of the "Titanic")' in 1915.

The disaster was made into a Nazi propaganda film in 1943 (*Titanic*) and an American melodrama in 1953.

Walter Lloyd brought out the novel *A Night to Remember* in 1955, which was brought to the big screen in 1958.

In a 1973 episode of *Upstairs Downstairs* Lady Marjorie Bellamy is lost on the *Titanic*, but her maid survives.

The 2007 Christmas special of *Doctor Who* had the Doctor on board an ill-fated spaceship named *Titanic*, which was set to collide with earth.

In the 2010 premiere of the ITV series *Downton Abbey*, the presumptive heir to Downton Abbey dies aboard *Titanic*.

And, of course, James Cameron's 1997/2012 film *Titanic*.

101. Timeline: Lest We Forget

30 MAY **2011**

★ ★ ★ ★ ★ ★ ★ ★ ★ ★ ★ ★ ★ ★ ★ ★ ★

A single flare was fired over Belfast docklands in commemoration of *Titanic*'s launch; boats around Harland and Wolff shipyard sounded their horns; the crowd applauded for exactly 62 seconds

15 APR **2012**

★ ★ ★ ★ ★ ★ ★ ★ ★ ★ ★ ★

Cruise ship *Balmoral*, which was charted to follow the original route of *Titanic* beginning in Southampton, stopped over *Titanic*'s resting place; another memorial cruise was conducted on *Azamara Journey*, which left from New York

10 APR **1912**

★ ★ ★ ★ ★ ★ ★ ★ ★ ★ ★ ★ ★ ★

SeaCity Museum, Southampton, was opened on the centenary of the ship's departure from the city

14
APR
2012

SEP
2012

FUTURE PLANS

BBC Radio 2 aired a 3-hour, minute-by-minute account of the disaster

In the first 6 months of opening in 2012, 500,000 people visited *Titanic* Belfast, and they came from 111 countries

An Australian billionaire has announced plans to recreate *Titanic* as *Titanic II*

Bibliography

Books

Behe, George, *On Board RMS Titanic* (2012)

Beveridge, Bruce & Hall, Steve et al., *Titanic: The Ship Magnificent*, Vol. 1 (2008)

Beveridge, Bruce & Hall, Steve et al., *Titanic: The Ship Magnificent*, Vol. 2 (2008)

Chirnside, Mark, *The Olympic Class Ships: Olympic, Titanic, Britannic* (2011)

Chirnside, Mark, *'Olympic', 'Titanic', 'Britannic': An Illustrated History of the Olympic Class* (2012)

Gibson, Allen, *The Unsinkable Titanic* (2012)

Gracie, Archibald, *Titanic: A Survivor's Story* (1985)

Hall, Steve & Beveridge, Bruce, *Titanic or Olympic?* (2012)

Halpern, Sam & Hall, Steve et al., *Report into the Loss of the SS Titanic: A Centennial Reappraisal* (2011)

Hutchings, David, *The Titanic Story* (2008)

Jessop, Violet, *Titanic Survivor: The Memoirs of Violet Jessop, Stewardess* (2007)

Klistorner, Daniel & Hall, Steve et al., *Titanic in Photographs* (2011)

Sheil, Inger, *Titanic Valour* (2012)

Websites

www.discovernorthernireland.com/titanic2012
www.encyclopedia-titanica.org
www.the-titanic.com/Home.aspx
www.titanic-nautical.com
http://stevehall.txc.net.au
http://centennial.titanicology.com
www.titanic-theshipmagnificent.com